8 X 11/05

Celebrations of Light

A Year of Holidays Around the World

Celebrations of Light

written by Nancy Luenn

illustrated by Mark Bender

ATHENEUM BOOKS FOR YOUNG READERS

In memory of Marianne Wolman, a light in my life
— N. L.

To my wonderful family
—M. B.

AUTHOR'S NOTE

This book describes twelve celebrations of light. Others include All Saints' Day and All Souls' Day in Europe, Latin America, and the Philippines; the Hungry Ghost Festival in China and Taiwan; Prachum Ben in Cambodia; and Tet in Vietnam.

For more information about festivals of light, see *The Folklore of World Holidays*, edited by Margaret Reade MacDonald (Detroit: Gale Research, Inc., 1992) and *Joy Through the World*, an Allen D. Bragdon Book produced in cooperation with the U.S. Committee for UNICEF (New York: Dodd, Mead and Co., 1985).

ABOUT THE MUSLIM CALENDAR

Muslims use a lunar calendar which is completely independent of the solar year. The Muslim months begin with each new moon. Each year, the Muslim month of Ramadan begins ten to twelve days earlier on the Western calendar than it did the year before.

This means that if the festival of Lanterns at the end of Ramadan takes place in January this year, two years later it will fall in December. Several years after that it will occur in November, and so on until it has circled the entire solar year over a thirty-two-year cycle.

Atheneum Books for Young Readers
An imprint of Simon & Schuster Children's
Publishing Division
1230 Avenue of the Americas
New York, New York 10020

Text copyright © 1998 by Nancy Luenn
Illustrations copyright © 1998 by Mark Bender

All rights reserved including the right of reproduction
in whole or in part in any form.

Book design by Angela Carlino
The text of this book is set in Cochin

The illustrations are rendered in airbrush.

First Edition
Printed in Singapore
10 9 8 7 6 5 4 3 2

Library of Congress Cataloging-in-Publication Data
Luenn, Nancy.
Celebrations of Light: a year of holidays around the
world / by Nancy Luenn ; pictures by Mark
Bender. — 1st ed.
p.   cm.
Summary: Describes various festivals centered around
light that are celebrated by different cultures

throughout the year, including Candlemas, Bon
Matsuri, Diwali, Hanukkah, Luciadagen,
and Kwanzaa.
ISBN 0-689-31986-X
1. Festivals — Juvenile literature. 2. Light — Religious
aspects — Juvenile literature. 3. Candles and lights —
Juvenile literature.
[1. Festivals. 2. Light — Religious aspects.] I. Bender,
Mark, ill. II. Title.
GT3933.L84   1998
394.2'6 — dc20   96-2761

Contents

INTRODUCTION

Long ago, people found a way to light the darkness. They built fires to keep warm and cook their food. They lit torches to drive away danger. To help them see at night, they learned to make candles and lanterns. Light was so important in their lives that they came to use it in worship and in celebrations.

For thousands of years, people have held festivals of light. Some of these festivals help brighten winter. Others welcome spring. Some light the way for a god or a goddess. Lights are kindled to honor the dead and to celebrate birth. Throughout the year, lights shine on special days.

Brazil

It is summer in Brazil on New Year's Eve. In Rio de Janeiro, people dress in white. They flock to the beaches at midnight. There they sing songs to Iêmanjá, African goddess of waters, and ask her for good fortune in the coming year. They offer perfume, combs and shells, and mirrors to reflect her beauty.

Hundreds of candles are set in the sand. Then people wade into the bay and scatter white flowers over the waves as a gift to Iêmanjá.

JANUARY—FEBRUARY

China and Taiwan

The Chinese New Year begins on the first day of the First Moon. Sweeping out the old year, people get ready for spring. They hold family reunions, visit friends, and show respect to gods and ancestors. The celebration lasts for fifteen days.

The last day of the New Year celebration is a festival of lanterns. Paper lanterns hang in temples, streets, and homes. The lanterns come in all shapes and sizes: dragons, airplanes, cars and fish, dragonflies and tigers. In Taiwan, it is said these lanterns welcome back the light of spring.

JANUARY
(MONTH VARIES)

Sierra Leone

People in Freetown celebrate Lanterns at the end of Ramadan, the Muslim holy month, according to the lunar year. In the 1930s, when this festival began, simple lanterns were paraded through the streets. Muslims carried them to celebrate the day that their prophet Muhammad received the Koran.

Over the years, the lanterns grew bigger as people competed to build the best one. Now, many of the lanterns are huge floats. Lit from within, these floats are pulled by vehicles or teams of men. Both Muslims and non-Muslims celebrate Lanterns. Together they dance and sing in the streets until dawn.

Luxembourg

Christians in many countries celebrate Candlemas on February 2. Forty days after Jesus was born, his mother, Mary, took him to the temple. There, a man named Simeon foretold that Jesus would become a "light of revelation." In some Christian churches, candles are blessed on this day.

In Luxembourg, this holiday is known as Lichtmesdag. When evening comes, children carry candles door to door. They sing a traditional song about light to their neighbors. The children are given candy and gifts for their song.

Korea

Koreans use lanterns to celebrate the Buddha's birthday. On the eighth day of the Fourth Moon, families visit Buddhist temples. Lanterns and paper flowers decorate the courtyards. Inside the temple, people burn incense and put flowers on the altar. They stand and pray for Buddha's blessings.

When night comes, they light more lanterns at their homes. In some towns, lanterns are paraded through the streets. These lanterns symbolize the light of Buddha's teachings.

Japan

In the middle of July or August, Buddhists in Japan hold Bon Matsuri. This festival honors the dead. Carrying lanterns, people go to graveyards to welcome their visiting ancestors. Incense, lanterns, and branches of *sakaki* and umbrella pine adorn the graves. More lanterns shine outside each home.

The ancestors visit for three days. They are offered food and are entertained with *bon-odori*, joyful dances. On the third night, people who live near the water invite their ancestors to leave in tiny boats. A lantern shines in each one. Slowly, the boats drift away, bearing the names of the ancestors.

India

Diwali, the Hindu festival of lights, is held in the Indian month of Kartika. Thousands of lights shine on houses, walls, pathways, streets, and riverbanks. These lights welcome Lakshmi, the goddess of wealth and good fortune. They guide her way to every home.

Women and girls take small clay lamps to the river. They light the oil in the lamps and set them afloat. If the lamps cross safely to the other side, it is seen as a sign of good fortune.

NOVEMBER

Thailand

Loy Krathong is a festival of floating lights. In Thailand, on the fifteenth day of the Twelfth Moon, people give thanks to Me Khongkha, the mother of waters.

Using paper or banana leaves, they make bowls in the shape of lotus blossoms. Incense, flowers, and a lighted candle are put inside each bowl. Hundreds of these *krathongs* are set afloat on lakes, canals, and rivers.

NOVEMBER—DECEMBER

Israel

Hanukkah celebrates a miracle of light. Two thousand years ago, determined Jewish men reclaimed their temple from a foreign army. When the priests went to light the menorah, they found only a night's worth of oil. They lit the sacred flame, and to everyone's amazement, the oil burned for eight days.

Jews remember this event each year by lighting a menorah. The first candle is lit on the twenty-fifth day of the Jewish month of Kislev. Each night another candle is added. On the eighth night, all the candles glow.

Sweden

On December 13, Swedes celebrate Luciadagen. Lucia was a Christian who died for her beliefs and was made a saint. Many years later, during a famine in Sweden, a peasant saw a vision of Lucia. Dressed in white and crowned with lights, she carried gifts of food. Her feast day became a special holiday in Sweden.

On Luciadagen, the oldest girl in each family dresses up as Lucia. On her head she wears a wreath of candles. She brings her parents breakfast in bed—saffron-flavored buns and hot coffee. Her brothers and sisters often go with her, dressed up as star boys and angels.

DECEMBER

United States and Mexico

Lights shine for Christmas, the birthday of Jesus. Electric lights twinkle in shop windows, on tree branches, and all along the eaves of houses. Inside, they glow on Christmas trees.

In the Hispanic Southwest, people make lights called *luminarias*. They put candles in paper bags weighted with sand. Rows of *luminarias* line rooftops, walls, and pathways. They light the way for *las posadas*. This is a candlelight procession of people enacting Joseph and Mary's search for an inn. They knock at the door of a relative's home. Singing, the people ask for shelter. At first they are refused, but at last their host welcomes them in.

United States

Beginning on December 26, many African-Americans light candles to celebrate Kwanzaa. Kwanzaa was created in 1966. It honors African harvest traditions and the values of the black community. Each night for a week a new candle is lit. The candles represent the seven principles of Kwanzaa: unity, thinking and acting for oneself, working together and helping one another, buying from one another and sharing the wealth, purpose, creativity, and faith.

During Kwanzaa, families and friends come together to enjoy their common heritage. Sharing the unity cup, they take pride in their culture and the strengths of their community.

All around the world there are festivals of light. The lights shine for all that is good in our lives. They honor wisdom, faith and love, and hopes for brighter days.

Lights used in celebration have a special glow. They warm our hearts and calm our fears. The candles on a birthday cake help count the years. They hold the secret of a wish.